Adler
Planetarium

Shedd
Aquarium

Buckingham
Fountain

Art
Institute

Field & Co.

Soldier
Field

Chicago
Meigs
Field

McCorm
Place Eas

41

Grant Park

Field Museum of
Natural History

Prairie Ave.
Historic
District

Prairie Ave.

Indiana Ave.

McCormick
Place West

University
of Chicago

Michigan Ave.

Wabash Ave.

State St.

18th St.

Adlai E. Stevenson Expwy.

Sears
Tower

LOOP

Adams St.

Jackson Blvd.

Randolph St.

Washington Blvd.

Clark St.

Congress Pkwy.

Roosevelt Rd.

S. Branch Chicago R.

CHINA-
TOWN

Cermak Rd.

Pullman
Historic
District

55

94

90

Comiskey Park

Canal St.

Halsted St.

GREEKTOWN

290

Washington Blvd.
Warren Blvd.

Archer Ave.

A PHOTOGRAPHIC TOUR
CHICAGO

A PHOTOGRAPHIC TOUR
CHICAGO

CAROL M. HIGHSMITH AND TED LANDPHAIR

Index

This neighborhood, about fifty blocks north of downtown, typifies the city's outer edge, just inside the suburbs. Many two- and three-bedroom brick homes, built in the 1940s and '50s, have been individualized with additions and prized plantings. Neighborhood kids are Chicago sports diehards in training, whose garb depends on the sport in season.

A gaggle of gargoyles adorns an entry gate to the University of Chicago (opposite), which sprawls across 184 acres of South Chicago. The university's medical, law, economics, and graduate schools are world-renowned. ABOVE: O'Gara and Wilson antiquarian booksellers in Hyde Park, near the University of Chicago, is known city-wide as a likely place to locate used and scarce scholarly books. OVERLEAF: The Museum of Science and Industry, the grande dame of Chicago's thirty-four museums, was built as the Palace of Fine Arts at the 1893 world expo. Its exhibits include a replica of a coal mine, a "whispering gallery," the Apollo 8 spacecraft, and the workings of a German submarine. Kids and adults alike gravitate to the Omnimax Theater, where movie scenes reach out and surround them, and to a pulsating, sixteen-foot model of the human heart.

"Public art" turns up in surprising places, including an "El" station on East Fifty-sixth Street. On this rather existential mural (left), people of diverse backgrounds address the question "Where are you going?" with answers such as, "Home, probably to be quiet with my wife and kids," and "It's not the most opportune time to discuss where I'm going spiritually. I mean, I'm giving a seminar on growth therapy. I'm on a different plane alto-gether." ABOVE: On South Lake Park Avenue, the Chevro-let Building, which once housed an auto-mobile dealership and was dramatically saved when most of the block was razed, includes beautiful terra-cotta details.

The Historic Pullman District (above), is a remnant of railroad-car maker George Pullman's "model town" in South Chicago. Its corner-stone is the Queen Anne-style Florence Hotel, built in 1881 and named for Pullman's favorite daughter. The nonprofit Historic Pullman Foundation operates the hotel—which is owned by the State of Illinois—as a museum and restaurant. The baron and his family used the Pullman Suite (right) when they visited from their Prairie Avenue home. OVERLEAF: Chicago sculptor Lorado Taft designed the Fountain of Time. It was dedicated in Hyde Park, near the University of Chicago, in 1922. The haunting statue's theme, suggested by a line from Austin Dobson, reads: "Time goes, you say? Ah no, alas. Time stays. We go."

Among the displays at the Polish Museum of America (above) on North Milwaukee Avenue is the re-created New York hotel room where incomparable pianist Ignaczi Paderewski lived and practiced his craft. The museum collects materials on the lives of Poles in America, including Revolutionary War hero Tadeusz Koscziusko. It also displays the Stations of the Cross from the first Polish church in America, which, curiously, was in Texas. Multiethnic Chicago also houses many other ethnic cultural centers, including the Balzekas Museum of Lithuanian Culture, the DuSable Museum of African American History, the Mexican Fine Arts Center, the Oriental Institute, the Swedish-American Museum, and the Ukrainian Institute of Modern Art. OPPOSITE: A variety of tongues can be heard in the city's churches, synagogues, and mosques as well. Holy Trinity Catholic Church, for instance, holds services in Polish.

Every summer in Chicago, there is a colossal mass food-sampling called the "Taste of Chicago." Even presidents of the United States have stopped by to sample the incredible assortment of ethnic and traditional American cuisine. But Chicagoans and visitors can avoid the crowds by simply hopping in their cars and driving along the city's main arteries, where the assortment of culinary options seems never-ending. The Polish influence is still strong in old Chicago, for instance, and bakeries like the Pasieka (right) on North Milwaukee Avenue, and restaurants such as the Busy Bee (above) on North Damen Avenue, offer delights fit for Warsaw. Notable at the Busy Bee are the czarina (duck gravy soup) and pierogis stuffed with meat and potatoes or potato and sauerkraut.

Chicago's Chinatown (top) south of downtown is compact. It is largely confined to South Wentworth Avenue but is loaded with gustatory gems. BOTTOM: Like deep-dish pizza, the hot dog is a Chicago artform, and it is prepared with panache (and any number of garnishes) at the Superdawg, a quirky drive-in on North Milwaukee Avenue. Further north of the city, as one nears the Wisconsin border, the influence of the bratwurst (as in a "brat and a beer") begins to be felt, but Chicago is old-fashioned frankfurter country. OPPOSITE: Mario's, on West Taylor Street, restricts its lemonade-making to the warm months.

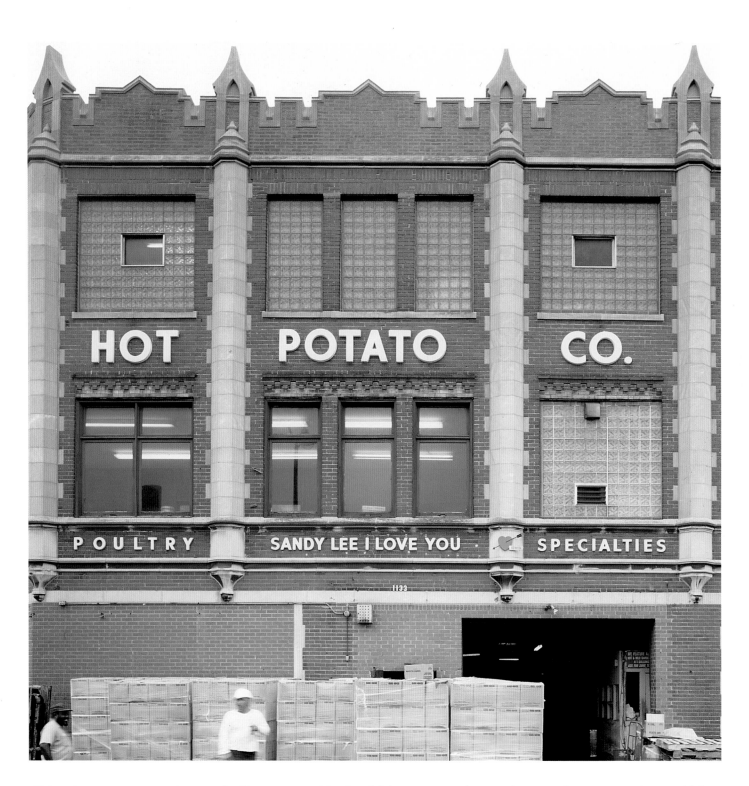

Chicago's unpredictable array of small businesses inspires double-takes and chuckles through clever signage and advertising. The All Ways Ink Tattoo Parlor (opposite) is located on Milwaukee Avenue; the Hot Potato Company (above), with its baffling "Sandy Lee I Love You" inscription above the door, and the lavishly designed Chicago Importing Company (overleaf) are on West Randolph Street. On these thoroughfares, and on Clark and Halsted streets, Clybourn and Broadway avenues, and Diversey Parkway, merchants seem to vie for the cleverest slogans and most creative outdoor designs, matching the sometimes-whimsical merchandise inside. Shoppers who prefer chain and outlet stores can find them mixed in with these unconventional emporiums. Add the ethnic flavor of the city's innumerable delis, bakeries, taverns, and corner restaurants, and you are confronted with an almost impossible choice of where to begin.

In his h
Lloyd W
to his ar
beliefs.
drafting
and fan
(opposi
his penc
plicity o
function
raised s
with hi
Cather
leaving
wife of
experi
styles a
here. F
buildin
in 1893
profess
where
one qu
life's w
includ
House
his ma
horizo
cantile
ribbon
windo
copiec
in hor
clients
The W
and S
owned
Natio
Histo

With student help, Lane Technical High School teacher Patrick Dawson sculpted— and teacher Ted Szalinski painted— this totem, Ignorance to Wisdom, *for the* school's golden jubilee in 1983. The highly-selective school has more than four thousand students. ABOVE: *Soldier Field, home of the Chicago Bears football team,* the Chicago Fire soccer team, and many other sporting and concert events, was originally built in the 1920s. In 2002, everything but the famous colonnade was destroyed to build a new stadium with more amenities, better parking, improved access for disabled patrons, and fun features like a sledding hill and children's playground. The project, which was part of a $587-million lake-front improvement plan, cost an estimated $365 million and only took twenty months to complete.

The fishing is fine at several spots along the lake (above). Perch, catfish, and trout are commonly caught, but there's an occasional salmon to be snagged as well. Tackle ranges from a simple line dropped off a pier to sophisticated casting rods that fling tempting morsels out into deep water. Those who keep their sailboats in the harbor can catch a lift to their boats from the Department of Recreation, which keeps its own boats at the dock (right). And the lakefront is home to some of the finest yachts on the Great Lakes (opposite). Sailboat lessons and rentals are available at several locations, though newcomers are advised that winds, shoals, and rocks along the shoreline can be tricky and sometimes treacherous.

Many cities across the
nation have enlisted
the help of developers
to turn harbors or
other sections into
festival marketplaces,
parkland, or recre-
ation districts in
order to add life to
downtown. But no
such efforts are
needed in Chicago,
which has a ready-
made playland on its
beaches, bike paths,
parks, and out on
Lake Michigan itself.
Weekdays, weekends,
and even many
evenings, there's

family activity on the
beach (above and
right). Chicago's
twenty miles of
beaches are open to
swimmers from
morning to sunset
during months when
the water tempera-
ture is bearable, and
some even have
changing facilities.
Beachgoers have a
busy scene in front of
them in the harbor
(overleaf), and those
who are out on the
water enjoy a spec-
tacular view of the
Chicago skyline.

Recreation along Lake Michigan's North Avenue Beach is both active and sedentary. Cyclists, in-line skaters, joggers, and skateboarders whiz past the Lincoln Park Chess Pavilion, which seems to attract players even on cool and misty days. Carved king and queen figures on each end of the 1950s-vintage pavilion inspire players. A spring ritual along the lakefront is the harvesting of smelt. Fishers—often whole families out for a nighttime diversion—attract the spawning creatures at night using small lights, and the shoreline during smelt season looks like a necklace of Chinese lanterns. ABOVE: Few other northern cities can offer so pleasant and expansive a beachfront as Chicago. But only the hardy brave the icy winds that swirl on the lakefront in winter.

The Lincoln Park Zoo (above), the nation's oldest zoological park, began in 1868 with the gift of a pair of swans. Now more than one thousand animals are exhibited. The zoo is an enthusiastic participant in "SSPs"— species survival plans, established by the American Zoo and Aquarium Association, designed to ensure the continued genetic diversity of animals in captivity throughout North America. The Lincoln Park Conservatory (right), north of the zoo, features palm, fern, and cactus houses. It mounts enormously popular azalea shows in February, Easter shows in March or April, crysthanthemum shows in November, and a lavish Christmas show in December. Lincoln Park is a testament to architectural ingenuity, as most of the park and its nearby residential neighborhood were underwater prior to 1860.

Dearborn Parkway (right), south of Lincoln Park, is one of the most refined of Gold Coast avenues. Apartment towers and low-rise office buildings have been tastefully integrated into the neighborhood of turreted brownstones. OPPOSITE: The Second City Comedy Club occupies a beautiful old building on North Wells Street. The legendary improvisational club was the training ground for comedians like Elaine May, Joan Rivers, John Belushi, Bill Murray, and Shelly Long. It spawned several branches, including one in Toronto that produced Dan Akroyd and John Candy. Chicago is also home to a half-dozen other comedy clubs, myriad jazz, dance, blues, and country-music clubs, as well as eclectic nightspots featuring everything from sambas to zither music.

Simple but delicious food is a Chicago obsession. Sports fans love the chumminess of the Billy Goat Tavern underneath the Chicago River Bridge. The restaurant was founded by William Sianis in 1934. He served goat cheese along with his burgers and fried onions, and newspaper writers took to calling him "The Goat." BOTTOM: A Chicago creation is deep-dish pizza, which Gino's East has been baking for more than thirty years. Founded by two cabdrivers, Gino's has a taxi motif, and customers are invited to add tasteful graffiti to most of the restaurant's walls. OPPOSITE: Harry Caray, the legendary Cubs baseball announcer, opened a restaurant in a historic building, designed by Henry Ives Cobb in 1900, on West Kinzie Street. Caray's beloved "Cubbies" often drop by.

The Bicycle Museum of America is one attraction at North Pier, an indoor shopping arcade in a converted warehouse on East Illinois Street. The museum offers a panoply of bikes, from early models to today's most sophisticated racing cycles. It sponsors long-distance bike tours and offers historical exhibits, such as the history of women in cycling. ABOVE: Most visitors enter the Museum of Contemporary Art building, which opened on East Chicago Avenue in 1996, on a grand staircase that is itself modern art. The building's German architect, Joseph Paul Kleihues, likens the stairway to the proylaea of the Acropolis and the step of the Altes Museum in Berlin. The museum and its sculpture garden, which were Kleihue's first U.S. project, rose in the shadow of the city's historic Water Tower on a site formerly occupied by a National Guard armory.

1897 Old Hickory

Tonk Manufacturing Co.,
Chicago

Tonk, like some other manufacturers, thought wood would be good for frames because it absorbed vibrations better than steel. Whether it had a smooth ride or not, the Old Hickory was beautiful, with its spare design and ornamental logo.

On loan from Schwinn Development Co.

The penthouse of the Executive Plaza Hotel offers an unusual view of movable bridges over the Chicago River, looking northwest toward Wolf Point. The "twin corncob" Marina City apartments were designed by Bertrand Goldberg from 1959 to 1967. To the river's left runs Wacker Drive, the nation's only downtown street that turns hard north, east, south, and west. ABOVE: The brilliantly lit, 1919 Wrigley Building, famous for its wedding-cake embellishments and clock tower, was long a symbol of dynamic Chicago. OVERLEAF: Navy Pier's Ferris wheel offers an animated perspective of the city skyline.

OPPOSITE: Edward Bennett designed the Defense relief on the Michigan Avenue Bridge in 1920. It commemorates the determination to rebuild Fort Dearborn on this site after Indians allied with British forces destroyed the fort and massacred most of its settlers during the War of 1812. LEFT: Chicago's beloved 1866 Water Tower, designed by William Boyington, anchors a lovely park on North Michigan Avenue. Horse-drawn carriages assemble around it, and the city maintains a visitor-information center there. The tower was part of an elaborate system in which water was pulled through tunnels from Lake Michigan and sent to a pumping station across the street. It was then pumped into the water tower, which helped equalize pressure so the water could be distributed to municipal water mains.

CITY OF CHICAGO

DEFENSE

Nearly everyone who spoke at the dedication of the Harold Washington Library Center in the South Loop in 1991 noted that the late Chicago mayor loved to read. The building blended uncannily with turn-of-the-century neighbors like the Old Colony Building and the city auditorium. The monolith immediately became the world's largest public library. ABOVE: Outdoor exhibitions of bronze sculptures in Grant Park, placed in early May and removed in late October, have become a Chicago tradition. The Department of Cultural Affairs has acquired, and creatively displayed, a vast public art collection. OVERLEAF: Chicago's reputation as the "Windy City" is earned, especially on East Wacker Drive along the river, even if the nickname actually resulted from the verbal windiness of the promoters of its world's fair.

The Union League
Club (above) is one
of Chicago's private
clubs still thriving as
places for business
rendezvous and in-
town overnight stays.
RIGHT: The 1926
Jewelers (later Pure
Oil) Building was
once the home of
several wholesale
jewelry showrooms.
Dealers could drive
into the building, and
a monstrous elevator
would carry them—
automobiles and

all—to their floors
as a measure against
theft. Gangster Al
Capone liked the
idea; he built a
balcony-level speak-
easy during Prohi-
bition. OPPOSITE:
The stairway beyond
the Palmer House
Hilton's grand lobby
reaches the entrance
to the fabled Empire
Room, once a sump-
tuous supper club
and later home to
some of Chicago's
most glittering galas.

The ubiquitous Daniel Burnham designed the one-million-square-foot home of the Field Museum of Natural History in Grant Park. Named for the museum's chief benefactor, Marshall Field I, the museum added two of the largest living land animals, two fighting bull elephants (left) in 1905 and 1906. ABOVE: At a whopping 42 feet long, Sue (named after the fossil-hunter who discovered her, Sue Hendrickson) is the largest, most-complete Tyrannosaurus rex fossil ever found. After the purchase of Sue for 8.4 million dollars in 1997, it took Field Museum preparators more than 25,000 hours to clean and prepare the fossil for exhibition.

Along with traditional German dishes, Berghoff's, a Chicago institution, offers its private-label beer and bourbon. In fact, the restaurant holds Chicago liquor license No. 1. During Prohibition, Berghoff's served near beer and "Bergo Soda Pop." LEFT TOP: One of the city's best-loved and most meticulously restored downtown structures is the Monadnock Building, designed by Burnham and Root in 1889 and nearly doubled in size by Holabird and Roche in 1893. Because the building is all masonry, with no steel skeleton, its walls are six feet thick at the base. BOTTOM: The prolific Burnham also designed Marshall Field's & Co.'s signature State Street store. Its founder coined the maxim "Give the lady what she wants!" Field's has restored the downtown store to its early splendor and opened several branches.

Tower are open to visitors. The Water Tower, in fact, is one nexus of the city's visitor-information services, offering maps and brochures in several languages. Chicago loves to compile unusual facts and statistics. A visitor can learn, for instance, that the city boasts fifty movable bridges and produced the first roller skates (1884), Cracker Jacks (1893), zipper (1896), envelopes with windows (1902), Hostess Twinkie (1930), pinball game (1930), spray paint (sometime in the late 1940s), and McDonald's "Golden Arches" (1955). Chicago even keeps track of the number of billions of Oreo cookies turned out by Nabisco at the world's largest cookie and cracker factory.

Union Station, which replaced the 1881 Pennsylvania Railroad Station, was the last of Daniel Burnham's train-terminal projects. He died before construction was completed in 1925; the project, passed on to the firm of Graham, Anderson, Probst & White, had been interrupted by World War I and took ten years to complete. Clad in Bedford limestone quarried in Indiana, Chicago Union Station is the only U.S. railroad station with a "double-stub" track layout. Metra commuter and Amtrak long-distance passenger trains approach the station from two directions, with most tracks dead-ending at the concourse. The grand staircase in the renovated and mechanically upgraded terminal was prominently featured in a bloody shootout between mob characters and the forces of the G-man Elliot Ness in the 1987 movie *The Untouchables*.

The Merchandise Mart, another protean structure, remains the world's largest commercial building. Built by Marshall Field in 1931 to house showrooms and offices for wholesale dealers of giftware, office furnishings, and business products, it was sold to Joseph P. Kennedy during the Depression. The mart encloses more than four million square feet, employs more than nine thousand people, and draws more than ten thousand tradespeople a day. Its trade floors are open only to dealers, architects, and designers, but the first two floors have been converted into a retail mall.

In the 1940s the Navy Pier at the mouth of the Chicago River was the world's largest "commercial and pleasure pier," with shopping promenades and an inspiring view of the Chicago skyline.

houses a more modernist art collection, including ties, clocks, artists' books, abstract paintings, and even T-shirts, was constructed on space previously occupied by the Chicago Avenue Armory. At the "MCA," even the grand staircase, which Kleihues likened to the propylaea of the Acropolis and the steps of the Altes Museum in Berlin, are art.

Chicago is also home to delightfully different galleries and exhibitions. The DuSable Museum of African American History offers performances of music and dance and a "know your heritage" quiz. The Oriental Institute Museum at the University of Chicago features a monumental statue of Pharaoh Tutankhamen and a forty-ton, winged Assyrian bull-man relief among its five galleries of artifacts from the ancient Near East. The city also contains the Polish Museum of America, the nation's largest Mexican museum, the Balzekas Museum of Lithuanian Culture, the Swedish-American Museum Center, and the Ukrainian National Museum. Visitors with even more eclectic interests can find the International Museum of Surgical Science, with an extensive collection of early microscopes, x-ray equipment, and displays about acupuncture; the Museum of Contemporary Photography; the Museum of Broadcast Communications; the Museum of Holography, filled with three-dimensional laser images; the Terra Museum devoted to American art; and a Museum of Floral Arts. There's the May Weber Museum of Cultural Arts, which displays puppets, ceremonial shawls, and even a teeth-blackening tray; a bicycle museum and virtual-reality "digital theme park" at the North Pier shopping arcade in a converted furniture warehouse; and two museums of Judaica.

A summer magnet is the Ferris wheel at the three-thousand-foot-long Navy Pier, built in 1916 for commercial shipping. And historic buildings like Union Station, the old Chicago & Northwestern train terminal, the Sun-Times Building, the Water Tower, and the Tribune

By the 1920s, Michigan Avenue was well established as the commercial spine of Chicago. This view southward from Chicago Avenue shows the results of the city's careful planning and eye for beauty.

its name from a wheeling, dealing temporary city hall that had once stood on the site. Root even had four crows, three of them laughing, carved into the imposts of the entrance arch. The building's most breathtaking interior space was a dynamic central court—a sensory starburst of marble, glazed brick, a translucent glass skylight, and serpentine stairs—that called to mind London's Crystal Palace. In time the building's owner would call upon avant-garde architect Frank Lloyd Wright for a makeover. Wright, who spent twenty of his most productive years in his suburban Oak Park home and studio developing the Prairie style of low-slung homes with unconventional horizontal lines and numerous windows, cloaked the building's dark ironwork in marble and replaced Root's electroliers with chandeliers.

William Le Baron Jenney, regarded as the "father of the skyscraper," improved the design of these buildings by supporting his creations (notably the Manhattan Building on South Dearborn Street) with an internal iron skeleton rather than ponderous external walls. But it was Louis Henri Sullivan who was the exemplar of the "Chicago School" of architects—renowned for their use of minimal but enticing ornamentation at ground and roof level, gridlike intersecting piers and spandrels, and wide windows. "Form," Sullivan preached, "follows function." On the Carson Pirie Scott & Company department store building on South State Street, for example, he rounded the corner entrance, surrounded the display windows with cast-iron decoration, and clad the building's steel frame in terra-cotta. Sullivan and Dankmar Andler had been the first to sink watertight chambers through the ooze to bedrock to give still higher buildings a firm footing.

Little but rubble was left of the "Bryan Block" at the northwest corner of Monroe and La Salle streets after the terrible Chicago fire. Many ruins, including exquisite architectural fragments, became landfill.

Of all these geniuses, Daniel Burnham was selected to orchestrate an effort that would announce that Chicago had not only recovered from the terrible Fire, but had also arrived as a city of global importance. He directed the beguiling World's Columbian Exposition in 1893, a world's fair that would celebrate, a year late, the four-hundredth anniversary of Christopher Columbus's "discovery" of America. The fair's gabby promoters first earned Chicago the nickname "The Windy City."

What emerged in bogs and lagoons along the lakefront south of the city was no less than a shimmering, neoclassical Beaux-Arts "White City," filled with wonders of electricity, transportation, horticulture, and manufacturing. Fourteen million Americans—one-fourth of the country's population—came to see the gleaming buildings, most of which were little more than temporary props, their ironwork frames covered in timber and "staff," a mock stone made of plaster, horsehair, and cement. At the Exposition's close, the public was invited to wander the grounds, picking apart the structures for souvenirs. The rabble set several, including the Casino and the Peristyle, ablaze, dashing any thought of somehow turning the fair site into a permanent attraction. One expo building, Charles B. Atwood's Palace of Fine Arts, constructed of brick, then covered in plaster to safeguard its great artworks, survived and became the first Field Museum of Natural History. In 1920 it was renovated to house the city's new science and technology museum.

But Jackson Park, the Museum of Science and Industry, the broad parkway on which the expo's Midway Plaisance had once housed the "Bazaar of Nations" (where a scandalous belly dancer named "Little Egypt" was the biggest draw), and remnants of landscape architect Frederick Law Olmsted's "Wooded Isle" were not the only legacy of the White City. Its utopian one hundred thousand homeless, and obliterating 17,450 structures. A Gothic stone water tower on North Michigan Avenue survived to become a symbol of the city's rebirth. It was during these harrowing times that Chicago's first gritty, motivational motto, "I Will," was literally put to the fire. Within six years, Chicago had erected masonry structures everywhere, including sixteen new hotels. Its new public library was set up in an empty water tank, with books donated by world notables, including Britain's Queen Victoria.

Those in the relatively new practice of architecture, itching for a commission, flocked to the burned-out city. Daniel Burnham and his partner, John Wellborn Root, were already there. They devised the idea of "floating" a high-rise building on a steel-and-concrete pier sunk in the city's spongy soil. Among their classic collaborations was the 1891 Monadnock Building on West Jackson Boulevard. Sixteen stories high, it became the world's tallest office building and is still the tallest wallbearing structure, with base walls six feet thick to support the enormous weight. The dim hallways of the refurbished Monadnock, with its gentle bays and purple-brown brick, today retain the gaslit look of a grainy private-eye movie, but its downstairs saloon and bagel shop—and convenient cut-through from Jackson to West Adams Street—assure plenty of traffic.

Root, the less flamboyant partner, had also designed another of Chicago's best-loved buildings, The Rookery on South La Salle Street. More than eighty thousand square feet of plate glass in six hundred windows girdled The Rookery's massive cherry-red brick and terra-cotta walls, which Root accented with Romanesque arches and Moorish and Venetian details. Officially named the Central Safety Deposit Company Building after its principal tenant, The Rookery got

Chicago's famous Water Tower survived the Great Fire. It was a critical component of the city's early water system. Its 138-foot standpipe provided enough pressure to distribute water throughout town.

CHICAGO. THE CITY OF THE BIG SHOULDERS, still "stormy, husky, brawling" as Carl Sandburg extolled it, still rolling up its sleeves and getting to work, though assuredly no longer "hog butcher for the world." Where ninety city blocks of pens and slaughterhouses once stood on the South Side, only Daniel Burnham's massive stone entrance portal remains in a nondescript industrial park. A century has gone by since ten thousand visitors a day came to watch brawny men with sledgehammers deliver the *coup de grace* to bellowing hogs and steers at the Armour and Swift operations of the Union Stock Yards. Chicago has put on considerable finery and a few airs. But this boisterous, boastful, teeming, remarkably scrubbed prairie city is still the big dog of the Heartland.

Chicago is a place of lush green parks (five-hundred-fifty-two citywide—many right downtown), of slate lake waters, of quirky black-and-white bands on the caps of cops. Of yellow taxis that keep a move on, orange reflections of sunsets off shimmering skyscrapers, sienna festival costumes, tan walls surprisingly free from the scrawls of "urban artists." Of red Bulls heads and Bears crooked "Cs" everywhere, elegant brownstone villas, blue beer signs in tavern windows. Of white snowflakes as early as September and as late as May, swirling across the river and up Michigan Avenue and soon mashed to gray; of neon rainbows along the Magnificent Mile and in the passenger tunnel of O'Hare International Airport; and thriving, polyglot neighborhoods.

Chicagoans love their superlatives—the nation's first skyscraper (the Home Insurance Company Building, 1885) and the first comprehensive municipal plan (Burnham again, 1909). Most Nobel laureates; world's largest private building (the Merchandise Mart with ninety acres of floor space); best hot dog and pizza. Largest indoor aquarium, one of the world's last free zoos, most massive outdoor food festival. Civilization's largest free library. Even the largest Tiffany dome anywhere, atop the old central library, which has been transformed into another first— a free municipal cultural and performing-arts center. Chicago even has the only river in the world that was trained to run backward; in 1900, using a system of locks, engineers turned the flow of the Chicago River, preferring to transport the city's sewage to St. Louis rather than into Lake Michigan. Tallest building? You bet: Sears Tower, agrees everyone in "Chicagoland."

Chicago's wind does not just whip or whistle or mournfully howl. It fairly screams off the plains and through the city's high-rise canyons. Stolid Chicagoans simply hitch up their scarves and bend to their tasks with the same good nature that they weather a summer hailstorm or another Cubs collapse. Sure, it's cold, but Chicago is so "livable." Who can doubt it, with thirty-four museums, well over six thousand restaurants, more than two hundred annual parades, twenty-nine miles of lakefront, including fifteen miles of bathing beaches, and eighteen miles of bicycle paths? Or unexpected delights, like a summer public-art program that plops down whimsical statuary—horses, rabbits, elephants, surreal human figures, and all manner of other bizarre bronze forms—into Grant Park and the city's airports and train station, sometimes by helicopter. How satisfying is it, too, to come upon what the *Tribune* calls "a patch of peace" in the courtyard of DuSable High School in the projects neighborhood of South Chicago. Designed by students and overseen by an architect, the "Urban Ecology Sanctuary" includes water pools; roaming chickens, pheasants, peacocks, and a goat; and a quiet corner to mourn the neighborhood's murdered children.

Of course Chicagoans are used to living in an outdoor sculpture and architecture arcade. Do they even notice, any longer, Alexander Calder's fifty-three-foot steel "flamingo" in the

Chicago graphic artist Robert Mark Melnick executed this twelve-foot-by-seven-foot oil painting of the Court of Honor from the 1893 World's Columbian Exposition. It is displayed in the main dining room of Berghoff's Restaurant on West Adams Street downtown. The "Great White City" set in motion a "City Beautiful" movement across the nation.

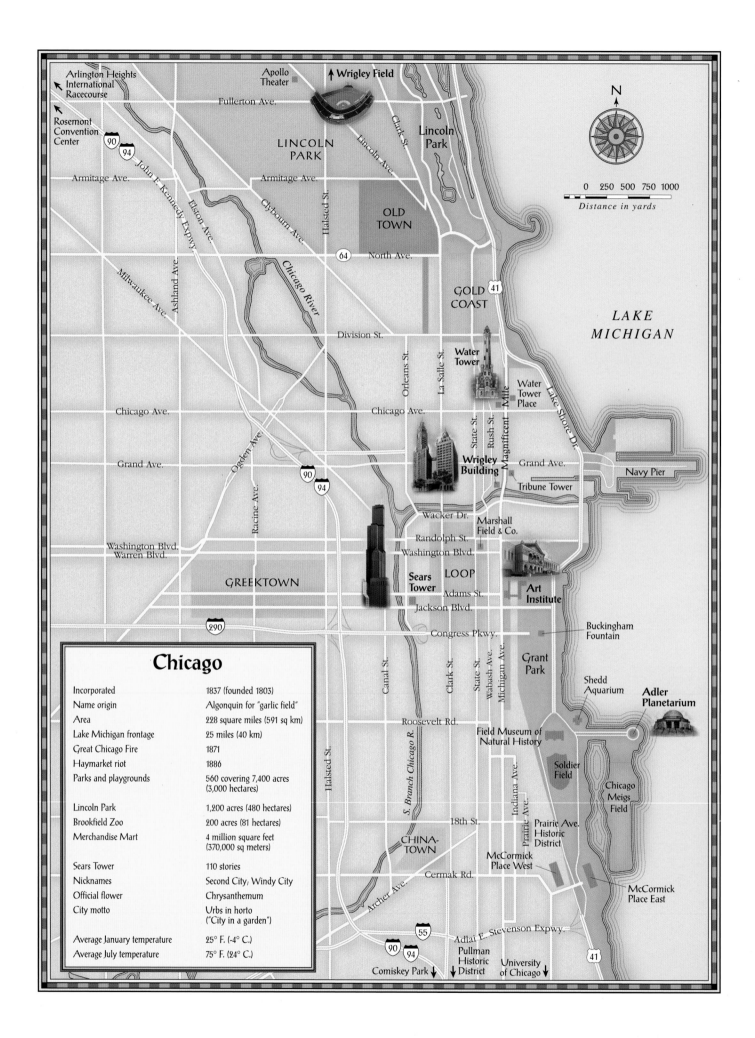

Wrigley Field

Apollo Theater

Arlington Heights International Racecourse

Rosemont Convention Center

Fullerton Ave.

LINCOLN PARK

Lincoln Park

N

Armitage Ave.

Armitage Ave.

John F. Kennedy Expwy.

Elston Ave.

Clybourn Ave.

Halsted St.

Lincoln Ave.

Clark St.

OLD TOWN

0   250 500 750 1000
Distance in yards

Milwaukee Ave.

Ashland Ave.

Chicago River

North Ave.

GOLD COAST

LAKE MICHIGAN

Division St.

Chicago Ave.

Ogden Ave.

Chicago Ave.

Water Tower

Orleans St.

La Salle St.

Water Tower Place

Grand Ave.

Grand Ave.

Racine Ave.

Wrigley Building

State St.

Rush St.

Magnificent Mile

Lake Shore Dr.

Tribune Tower

Navy Pier

Wacker Dr.

Marshall Field & Co.

Washington Blvd.
Warren Blvd.

Randolph St.

Washington Blvd.

Sears Tower

LOOP

Art Institute

GREEKTOWN

Adams St.

Jackson Blvd.

Buckingham Fountain

Grant Park

Congress Pkwy.

Canal St.

Clark St.

State St.

Wabash Ave.

Michigan Ave.

Shedd Aquarium

Adler Planetarium

Chicago

Incorporated	1837 (founded 1803)
Name origin	Algonquin for "garlic field"
Area	228 square miles (591 sq km)
Lake Michigan frontage	25 miles (40 km)
Great Chicago Fire	1871
Haymarket riot	1886
Parks and playgrounds	560 covering 7,400 acres (3,000 hectares)
Lincoln Park	1,200 acres (480 hectares)
Brookfield Zoo	200 acres (81 hectares)
Merchandise Mart	4 million square feet (370,000 sq meters)
Sears Tower	110 stories
Nicknames	Second City; Windy City
Official flower	Chrysanthemum
City motto	Urbs in horto ("City in a garden")
Average January temperature	25° F. (-4° C.)
Average July temperature	75° F. (24° C.)

Roosevelt Rd.

Field Museum of Natural History

Soldier Field

Chicago Meigs Field

Halsted St.

S. Branch Chicago R.

Indiana Ave.

18th St.

Prairie Ave.

Prairie Ave. Historic District

CHINA-TOWN

McCormick Place West

Cermak Rd.

McCormick Place East

Archer Ave.

Adlai E. Stevenson Expwy.

Pullman Historic District

Comiskey Park

University of Chicago

A BARNES & NOBLE BOOK

Text ©1997 by Random House Value Publishing, Inc. This edition 2004 by Barnes & Noble Publishing, Inc. by special arrangement with Random House Value Publishing, Inc.

ISBN 0-7607-5689-9

1 3 5 7 9 10 8 6 4 2

Project Editor: Donna Lee Lurker
Designed by Robert L. Wiser, Archetype Press, Inc., Washington, D.C.

All photographs ©1997 by Carol M. Highsmith unless otherwise credited:
page 5: map by XNR Productions;
page 6: painting by Robert Mark Melnick;
pages 8-21: Harold Washington Library Center;
Page 22-23: ©Richard Cummins;
page 37: ©Craig Lovell/Corbis;
page 83: ©Alan Schein/Corbis;
page 74-75: ©Richard Cummins/Corbis

Printed and bound in China by SNP Leefung Printers Limited.

THE AUTHORS GRATEFULLY ACKNOWLEDGE THE SUPPORT PROVIDED BY THE FOLLOWING IN CONNECTION WITH THE COMPLETION OF THIS BOOK:

HILTON HOTELS CORPORATION
AND
THE PALMER HOUSE HILTON

BARNES
& NOBLE
BOOKS

NEW YORK